THE WORLD'S HEARTBEAT

By Howard Gutner

CELEBRATION PRESS
Pearson Learning Group

CONTENTS

WHAT IS PERCUSSION?

Stop for a moment and listen to the sounds around you. What can you hear? Do you hear the ticking of a clock or the engine of a passing car? Perhaps it is raining, and you can hear the patter of raindrops beating against the window or hammering on the roof.

Thousands of years ago, people listened to the sounds around them just as you do today. They listened to the sound of rain as it beat down upon the earth. They heard the roar of thundering hooves as herds of animals stampeded over plains. They listened to the rush of a river or the crash of thunder as rain clouds collected in the sky. They noted the rhythm and sound of their work as they chopped wood, broke stones, or hoed the ground.

Soon people started to imitate the sounds around them by making sounds of their own. They clapped their hands and stamped their feet. They used sticks and stones to make sounds that resembled the sounds they heard in nature.

This is how instruments that people shake, hit, or scrape were invented. Today we call them **percussion** instruments. It's impossible to determine which culture invented them, but it's probably safe to say that at

This ancient Aztec drum has been carved from stone.

some point in nearly every **civilization**, somebody hit something, liked the sound, and decided to hit it again.

As time passed, these early percussion instruments became more complicated. People discovered that if they banged on a piece of wood, they made one kind of sound. If a tree trunk was hollowed out and a piece of animal hide was stretched over it, the sound was even better—deeper and much louder. Instruments like these were even used in prehistoric times.

The drum was one of the first musical instruments ever invented, probably because it is very easy to make. A thin skin, or membrane made of animal skin or plastic, is stretched over a simple hollow frame. Sound is made when the membrane is tapped with hands or fingers. This tapping makes the skin shake, or vibrate, with tiny movements.

When the membrane vibrates, it causes the air around it to vibrate also. These air vibrations are called sound waves, and when they spread down into the hollow part of the drum, they echo and grow louder. The vibration of sound waves is called resonance. It is the resonance that people hear when a drum is played.

The resonance can produce a high or a low sound, depending on where the membrane is struck or how tight it is stretched. In Africa and India, drum makers rub a small patch of paste onto the membrane of a drum. When the player beats on this special patch, the sound that it makes is lower than in other places on the membrane. In Africa this paste is usually made out of beeswax and roasted peanut powder. In India drum makers use rice and ashes.

Drums are made all over the world, usually with whatever materials people can find nearby. Most drums are made of wood, but in Arctic regions, in which there are no trees, the Inuit people use animal bone to make the drum frame. Drums can also be made out of clay or stone and many different types of metal, such as brass, copper, or steel.

Drums also come in many different sizes and shapes, but throughout the world, there are six main shapes. These shapes are pictured and described on the chart on the next page.

DRUM	DESCRIPTION
BARREL DRUM	Barrel drums are among the largest drums made. They often have a membrane at each end so they can be played on either side. Barrel drums with only one membrane are often large enough to be stood upright and played.
WAISTED DRUM	Waisted drums get their names because they are narrow in the middle and wide at the top and bottom. They can also have a membrane at one or both ends.
KETTLE DRUM	Kettle drums are shaped like a bowl or pot. They also have a single membrane and are sometimes called vessel drums because vessel is an old word for a cooking pot.
FRAME DRUM	Frame drums have one membrane, which is stretched over a very shallow frame, usually round.
GOBLET DRUM	Goblet drums are shaped like a drinking glass. They have a narrow base to support them on the ground and a wide membrane at the top.
LONG DRUM	Long drums are tall and thin and have a single membrane.

Just as there are different kinds of drums, there are also different ways to play them. You already know that you can strike a drum with fingers or hands. Large drums, however, are usually played with drumsticks, or beaters. Some beaters are made with wire brushes, which make a swishing sound when they hit the drum membrane. Other beaters have padded ends. The padding on the heads of beaters can be made from many different kinds of materials, including felt, leather, rubber, cork, or wood. A padded beater makes the sound of a drum soft and muffled. For a hard, crashing sound, beaters with no padding are used.

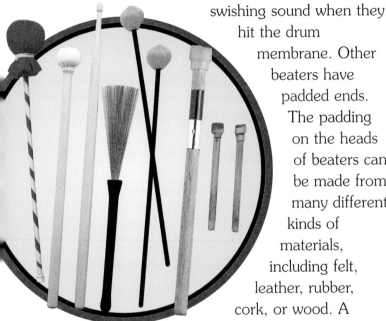

Drum beaters are made of different materials to make different sounds.

Whether a kettle or a barrel drum is played, and whether beaters or hands are used, all drummers produce a strong **repetitive** pattern of sound. This repeated pattern is called a rhythm.

When people march in a parade, their feet move in a particular rhythm. This marching rhythm could be written down as a short piece of music. A mark called a note would represent every step the marchers take. The notes would look like the top row of music below. Every section, or **measure**, contains two notes. These notes are called pulses, or beats, and they are the heartbeat of all music.

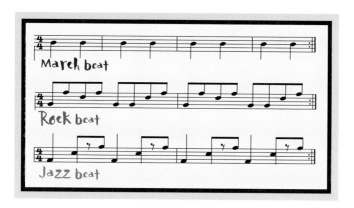

Just as some multisyllabic words put more **stress** on one syllable, certain notes in a piece of music are also stressed. These notes are called accented notes. A march that has a *one*-two, *one*-two beat tells that the accented notes are the first notes in each measure. A rock-and-roll song often stresses the first of four beats. By listening carefully to some songs, a person might count how many beats there are in a measure.

If people place their hands on their chests, they can feel their hearts beating like a marching rhythm. People can hear the beat in music just by using their ears and listening. Most music that is written in the United States has a rhythm of two or three beats. Much of the music written in Africa and Asia does not follow the same rhythm patterns as music written in the United States and Europe. Whatever rhythm pattern they follow, there is one thing musicians all over the world have in common—they all hear the beat of a drum.

Drums have been played to accompany dancing and in religious ceremonies. Some cultures still use a drumbeat to send messages, whereas others have pounded drums to scare their enemies on the battlefield. In Europe during the 1500s, drums were even used by dentists. When a patient was having a tooth pulled, a drum was used to drown out that person's yells!

Drums were among the first musical instruments that people created. Now, music played in most countries and cultures around the world includes some kind of drum or other percussion instrument.

CEREMONIAL DRUMS

In 3,000-year-old Egyptian tomb paintings, women musicians can be seen rattling dried plants, clapping their hands, and playing rectangular frame drums. Many women, called priestesses, played these instruments in Egyptian temples to honor their gods. Today, many thousands of years later, drums are still used in many cultures for **sacred** purposes.

In a 3,000-year-old tomb painting, a young woman plays an ancient Egyptian frame drum.

In North America, drums are an important part of Native American powwows. The meaning of the word *powwow* has changed over the years. Originally, in the language of the Native American Algonquian people, *pauwau* meant "medicine man," and *pau wauing* meant "a religious ceremony." In the 1800s, white settlers began to use the word to describe any gathering of Native Americans, whether it was a war dance, a victory celebration, or a meeting. Soon the word *powwow* was adopted by Native Americans, who now use the word to mean an event that celebrates their culture.

In many Native American traditions, the beat of the drum symbolizes a heartbeat. The drum and all of its parts are sacred, and drummers consider it a gift from their gods to be able to play it. In some families, the drums used in ceremonies have been handed down from generation to generation.

The most important part of any powwow is the drum. The drumheads used by Native Americans in powwows may be made of animal hides, usually from deer, elk, horse, buffalo, or cow. A Native American drum group (called simply "drum") is made up of as many people as can fit around a large drum. Usually the drummers at a powwow are men. According to the traditional beliefs of some groups, the gift of drumming was given only to men, just as the gift of beadwork was given to women. It is a great honor to be asked to drum at a powwow ceremony.

As the drummers beat the drum in unison, a lead singer starts the singing. Women often stand behind the drum group and sing along with the drummers. The singers have to know many different types of songs to accompany different dances.

Then the dancing begins. Some drum players at a powwow like to play trick songs, which cause dancers to miss a beat. Good dancers try to learn the songs of each drum group so they won't make a mistake. Their last step must match the last beat of the drum.

Some dancers at a powwow wear outfits made of animal skins and feathers to honor animals and birds, dancing in imitation of the creatures' movements. Other traditional dances are performed to give thanks or to honor ancestors. Sometimes dancers and drums compete.

Although the dances and songs at a powwow vary in style, rhythm, and pace, they all revolve around the beat of the drum. The beat unites everyone at a powwow and can often be heard late into the night.

Drummers perform at a powwow in Oklahoma.

DRUMS ON THE BATTLEFIELD

When people hear the beat of a drum, their energy levels rise. Long ago, people found that drumbeats could be used to energize soldiers and frighten their enemies.

In ancient times, along with all the loud noise the soldiers made, drums were often used to terrify the enemy. The ancient Egyptians always positioned drummers in the center of their attack force. The drummers were there to frighten the enemy and to keep energy levels high, while trumpeters were used for communication between units.

The use of war drums faded with ancient times, but it was revived in the Middle Ages when Christian armies from Europe met Muslim soldiers near the city of Jerusalem. The Europeans were shocked by the cacophony of noise the Muslims made as they went into battle with trumpets, drums, cymbals, and pipes. It did not take the Europeans long to adopt many of these instruments and put them to use on the battlefield.

Over the next few centuries, the armies developed the art of the drum in Western culture. The barrel drum arrived in the 1300s, followed by the side drum, and a few centuries later, the **bass** drum.

Drummers in Civil War regiments were young. This boy marched with the Union army.

Communication between soldiers is very important during a battle. They must know when to charge or march, retreat from an enemy, or hold their ground. Drum signals became an easy way for commanders to get this information to their troops. As a result, drummers became very important members of most European armies. Many became officers, and over time, a drummer's guild was formed in many countries. These guilds were a kind of club whose members voted to decide who was permitted to become a drummer in the armed forces. Men were chosen only from noble families, and most were required to undergo many years of training.

As Europeans began to **colonize** North and South America, the use of military drums spread across the Atlantic Ocean. During the American Revolution, British drummers controlled the rhythm of the battle, urging their troops into action against the Continental army.

Today, if you watch a marching band in a parade, you will likely see two types of drums. Both of them were developed from European military instruments. Huge bass drums can be up to 24 inches wide. They have a calfskin or plastic membrane on each side. The drummer wears the drum in front of the body hooked to an aluminum, fiberglass, or magnesium frame that fits over each shoulder. In a parade, a bass drummer usually gives the signal to a marching band to start and finish playing.

The snare drum you see in parades today looks very much as it did in the 1400s, when it became popular in Europe. It is still carried in the same way, too—on a sling that holds it in place on the drummer's left side, just below the waist.

The top of the snare drum is called the batter head because this is the side that is struck by sticks, or beaters. Underneath the drum is a set of wires called the snare, stretched across the head, that give the drum its name. They are designed to rattle against the lower head to make a biting, crashing sound every time a drummer strikes the batter head. To stop the snares

Parade drummers play large snare drums to keep the band marching in step.

from vibrating, a drummer presses a lever at the side of the drum, which loosens the snares. Then, when the membrane is struck by beaters, the drum produces a hard, strong sound.

A snare drum can probably make more different kinds of sounds than almost any other drum. For example, if a drummer plays it with wire brushes—sliding them across the drumhead—the snare produces a dry rustling sound. It reminds some people of leaves blowing in the wind or of two people whispering to each other.

To find drums that really *talk*, a person must travel to Africa! Drums in parts of Africa have long been used almost like telephones.

THE TALKING DRUMS OF AFRICA

In English, many words can have the same pronunciation and yet have two different meanings. For example, the words *here* and *hear* sound the same, but they have different spellings and different meanings. In some languages around the world, a word with the same spelling can be spoken in different tones to give two completely different meanings. If someone says a word in a high tone of voice it means something completely different from the same word spoken in a low tone of voice.

Yoruba, which is spoken in northern Nigeria, is one such language. Words in Yoruba go up and down like music. The same word, spoken in a different tone of voice, can have a different meaning. For example, the word *ilu* has two syllables. If someone pronounces the first syllable in a low tone of voice, and the second syllable in a high tone, the word *ilu* means "town." However, if a person pronounces each syllable in a low tone of voice, the word means "drum."

The Yoruba people use these same tones to send messages with drums. They use a large drum, called an *iya ilu*, for the low tones. A small drum, called a *kanango*, produces high tones. Some Yoruba drummers are so good they can send messages using one medium-sized drum called a *kerikeri*. How do they change the tones so that they can send messages with their drums?

The Yoruba drummers change the tone of a drum by changing the **tension** of the membrane. A tight membrane produces a high tone, and a loose one produces a low tone. In this way, a drummer can send messages to people many miles away.

The membrane can be attached to the body of the drum, using glue, nails, or lacing. The talking drums of Nigeria are laced very simply. As the drummer strikes the instrument with a beater, he adjusts the

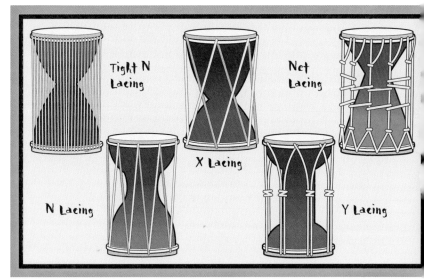

Lacing Patterns on Talking Drums

Drummers from the Yoruba in Nigeria play their talking drums.

lacing with his other hand. He pulls on the lacing to make the membrane tighter or looser, depending on the sound he wants to make.

Drummers in Nigeria can spread good news or warn people of danger with their drums. For a happy occasion, such as a wedding, the *ilu* is used to accompany dances. Many years ago, when tribespeople gathered to prepare for war, the *ilu* was used to tell stories about the heroic actions of their ancestors in order to strengthen the courage of the soldiers.

In Ghana, located west of Nigeria, the Ashanti

people also make talking drums, but tradition says that only a chief, or ruler, may own them. The drums are carved out of cedar wood. When a new drum is made, the drum maker first breaks an egg against the trunk of a tree, then addresses the tree, asking for permission to cut it down. The wood of one cedar tree will make many drums.

The Ashanti call their talking drums *atumpan* drums. A drummer may play two drums at the same time. The smaller drum has a high tone, whereas the larger one has a low, booming sound. Between them, the two *atumpan* drums imitate the spoken words of the Ashanti language.

Ashanti drummers in Ghana, West Africa, play atumpan drums.

Drums have been used to send messages, move troops across a battlefield, and honor ancestors. However, most drums today are used to make music. Almost every culture has a kind of music that uses drums. Here are just a few examples.

INDIA

Some people feel that the drummers of India are the best in the world. Most musicians in India use a pair of drums called the *tabla*. The larger drum has a metal body and is called a *bhaya*. The smaller drum, called a *daina*, is made of wood. The *daina* can always be found on the drummer's right-hand side and the *bhaya* on the left. The sound each drum makes can be changed in other ways besides spreading paste over the drum's membrane as described on page 5. Sometimes a drummer will place small blocks of wood under the lacing of the *tabla* to make the membrane tighter and the tone of the drums higher.

Playing the *tabla* can be complicated! Drummers usually play in a group. They squat on the ground and place the drums on their laps. They play each drum on its own and both drums at the same time, using one hand or both hands at the same time. The drums are

Master drummer Alla Rakha plays the tabla.

played in a rhythm called a *tala*. Most Western music
has two or three beats in a measure. In a *tala*
rhythm, there can be anywhere from 3 to 100 beats
in every measure! Indian drummers not only have
complicated rhythms to learn, they have to move fast!

JAPAN

In Japan, one of the oldest forms of music is called
gagaku. It is the official music of the Japanese
emperor and is played in the **imperial** court. In *gagaku*
music, drums are important to provide a background of
strong beats to keep the melody moving along to the
right rhythm.

Five kinds of drums are used to play *gagaku*
music: the *tsuri-daiko*, the *kakko*, the *ik-ko daiko*,
the *san-no-tsuzumi*, and the *da-daiko*.

The *tsuri-daiko* hangs from a decorated wooden or metal stand and is played with two sticks. Besides court music, it is also used in parades and festivals. The *kakko* drum rests on a low stand and has two membranes, one at each end. The drummer is usually seated and hits both ends of the drum. The *ik-ko daiko* is the only drum that is carried and played by a dancer. The *san-no-tsuzumi* is played by the leader. Although two-headed, only one side of the drum is played.

The *da-daiko* is a huge drum. No one who hears it will ever forget the sound. The drum is often set in a large, decorated frame on a special platform. Da-daiko drums are always played in pairs, placed side-by-side. The drums make a deep booming sound that moves across a room like an echo.

A bugaku drummer plays the *da-daiko,* or great drum.

23

SOUTH AMERICA

The music of South America, especially Brazil, is so famous for its energetic rhythms that a number of dances have been named after them. The rumba, the samba, and the bossa nova are South American dance rhythms that are played on two very special kinds of drums. The smallest of these is a pair of drums called bongos, which are usually held between the knees and are played with both the fingers and the hands, producing a high, tapping kind of sound. One drum is bigger than the other, so they play different notes.

Barrel-shaped conga drums are the largest hand drums in a South American band. Like the bongo, they are played with fingers or cupped hands. They make a full, deep sound.

A father and son play the congas.

THE MODERN DRUM

Drummers in countries around the world usually play only one kind of drum at a time. A drummer playing bongos could not play the conga drum at the same time. One person playing alone could never beat on the *tsuri-daiko* as well as the *kakko*. The drums might be played at the same time with each drum played by a different person.

In the United States, at the beginning of the twentieth century, most drums were also played as separate instruments by different people, usually while the player was standing up or marching. In a theater **orchestra**, though, a lack of space and money often meant that drummers had to play as many different instruments as they could. Many drummers developed a method called double drumming, which means that one drummer played both the bass drum and the snare drum.

Around the end of World War I in 1918, there was a great demand for musicians and orchestras in the United States. In large, big-city movie theaters, orchestras were hired to accompany silent movies. Bands were also employed in hotels so that people could dance before and after dinner.

Jazz, a type of American music that had begun in

the late 1800s, became increasingly popular as well. Jazz had its beginnings in the music of African Americans, including the drums used by the Yoruba and other African people. Jazz blended the rhythms of African music with American folk music and European popular music to make an exciting new sound.

By the 1920s, jazz and dance-band drummers in the United States wanted to put a group of drums together into a set that could be played by one person. They also wanted to include other instruments such as the cymbal, a brass plate that makes a loud ringing sound when it is struck. This group of percussion instruments would eventually be called a drum kit.

The device that made a modern drum kit possible had actually been invented years earlier. It was a simple idea that permitted the bass drum to be played in a brand new way.

In 1909, a drummer and inventor in Chicago named William Ludwig came up with a simple device called a foot pedal. Fastened to the bottom of a bass drum, Ludwig's foot pedal had a beater attached to it and a spring that automatically returned the beater to its starting position. As a result, a drummer could play a bass drum with one foot. In this way, drummers gained speed, and at the same time, freed

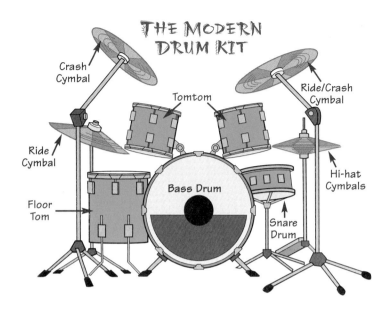

THE MODERN
DRUM KIT

Crash Cymbal

Tomtom

Ride/Crash Cymbal

Ride Cymbal

Bass Drum

Hi-hat Cymbals

Floor Tom

Snare Drum

their arms to play other instruments.

By 1910, William Ludwig and his brother Theobald were making foot pedals for most drummers in Chicago. They soon formed their own company with their sister Elizabeth and began making drums as well. By 1926 they were selling more than a million dollars' worth of drums and foot pedals a year across the United States, and their invention soon spread around the world.

The development of the foot pedal paved the way for the modern drum kit. Drummers could now sit before a set of drums and use a foot pedal to pound out the beat on the bass drum and sticks or beaters to play the snare, the cymbals, and other drums at the same time.

In the 1920s, drummers like Warren "Baby" Dodds and the Hot Seven jazz band made the drum kit popular across the United States.

In the 1920s, pioneer drummers, such as Warren "Baby" Dodds, began using drum kits. Dodds got his start playing in parades in New Orleans, and the first drum kits from the early 1920s contained the kind of large bass drums that were often carried in parades.

By the 1930s, drummers were playing drum kits that looked much like the drums rock musicians play today. They usually included a bass and snare drum, as well as two or three tom-tom drums. The tom-tom in a modern drum kit is a single-headed drum without any snares. Small tom-toms are often placed on top of the bass drum in a drum kit. Large ones, called floor toms by drummers, are fixed to a stand. The tom-tom is used to make sounds that resemble the sounds made by Native American and African drums.

The modern drum kit also usually includes at least

two kinds of cymbals. A hi-hat cymbal is operated by pressing a pedal that lowers or pulls one of the cymbals and allows it to crash onto the other cymbal when the pedal is released. A crash cymbal is attached to a long pole, and the drummer strikes it with a beater in much the same way as a drum is struck. The sound is a quick splash. Many drum kits also have a ride cymbal, which is thicker and larger than the crash cymbal and makes a clear pinging sound.

Drummers who use a drum kit in a rock or jazz band need a lot of energy and a lot of skill as well. They have to play as many as five or six drums, rushing from one instrument to the other with amazing speed. Watching a good drummer play a drum kit often turns out to be quite a show. With the increasing popularity of jazz and dance music in the 1920s and 1930s, many talented drummers became famous. Drummer Gene Krupa, who played with orchestra leader Benny Goodman and others, became a star around the world.

In 1927, Krupa also made history when he became the first drummer to make a record while playing a bass drum that had a foot pedal attachment. At first, the head of the record company told Krupa that he didn't want him to use the bass drum during the recording because it would be too loud. "I'm afraid the bass drum and those tom-toms will knock the needle off the wax and into the street," he told Krupa. That didn't happen. Instead, everyone discovered that the excitement of the drum could be captured on records.

Along with William Ludwig and Baby Dodds, Gene Krupa is also considered to be one of the founders of the modern drum kit. In 1935, Krupa talked H. H. Slingerland, of the Slingerland Drum Company, into making a tom-tom drum that could be tuned. In fact, it was tuned in much the same way as the drums used by the Yoruba in Africa were tuned. Drummers were then able to tighten or loosen the membrane and change the sound of a drum. These tunable tom-toms were first introduced in 1936, and they quickly caught on.

When rock music began to grow in popularity after 1955, drummers such as Ringo Starr of The Beatles, Keith Moon of The Who, Stewart Copeland of The Police, Phil Collins of Genesis, and Chad Smith of Red Hot Chili Peppers followed in Gene Krupa's footsteps. Each of them became famous for his unique way of playing the drums.

William Ludwig's drums, first manufactured in the 1920s, also became famous. The Ludwig company first became the world's largest drum maker. Then, more than 40 years later, Ludwig drums became well known to the public after Ringo Starr played on a set of Ludwig drums when The Beatles made their first American TV appearance in 1964.

Phil Collins is well known for his sense of timing and for being a left-handed drummer.

Over many thousands of years, people have continually invented and reinvented the drum. Whether it is carved out of a simple tree trunk or made from brass, steel, or copper, the drum is one of the oldest musical instruments and also one of the most popular. Its beat has called soldiers to battle and has lifted their spirits. It has coaxed people out onto the dance floor and has sent messages of warning and celebration. It has been played for emperors in their palaces and by kids pounding on an overturned can on the sidewalk.

The drumbeat is our heartbeat, and it will always be with us. The sound of a drum is an ancient sound and yet is as new as tomorrow.

GLOSSARY

bass	having low, deep sounds or tones
civilization	countries or peoples who have developed a written language, government, and arts and sciences
colonize	to start a colony, which is made up of a group of people who settle in a distant land but is still under the rule of the country from which it came
imperial	of an empire, or group of countries or territories, under the rule of another country
jazz	a kind of American music that originated with African American musicians in the South; it has strong rhythms and the players or singers originally could make up parts as they play
measure	the notes or rests or both between two bars on a staff of music
orchestra	a large group of musicians playing together; usually includes strings, wind, and percussion instruments
percussion	a musical instrument in which the tone or sound is made by striking or scraping some part of it, or by shaking it
repetitive	sounded or performed again and again
sacred	having to do with religion or worthy of reverence
stress	special force given a syllable, word, or note in speaking or in music
tension	the act of stretching or being stretched
tone	one of a series of sounds in music or voice; the difference in pitch, higher or lower, between one sound or note and another sound or note